Braiding

Braiding

Poems by

Susan Castillo Street

© 2022 Susan Castillo Street. All rights reserved.
This material may not be reproduced in any form, published,
reprinted, recorded, performed, broadcast,
rewritten or redistributed without
the explicit permission of Susan Castillo Street.
All such actions are strictly prohibited by law.

Cover design by Shay Culligan

ISBN: 978-1-63980-129-9

Kelsay Books
502 South 1040 East, A-119
American Fork, Utah 84003
Kelsaybooks.com

To David

and to Isabella, Mariana and Martim

Acknowledgments

Button Eye Review: "Joan" and "Bogotá"

In *The Gun-Runner's Daughter,* Kelsay Press: "Permanent Damage"

Dreich: "My Life in Cars," "Hair Haiku," and "Cliffhanger"

Obsessed with Pipework: "Cross Words"

Allegro: "Dark Ghosts"

Ink Sweat and Tears: "Witches' Broom" and "Winter Roses"

Locked Down: Poetry, Diaries and Art from the 2020 Pandemic, Poetry Space: "Plagued" and "Clap for Carers"

Poetry and Covid: "Webs" and "White Raven on My News Feed"

Highly Commended in *Poetry on the Lake:* "Plague Saint"

Prole: "Que las hay, las hay"

Up!: "Fairy Hunting"

Caduceus: "Visions"

Fragmented Voices: "Braiding" and "Bloom Where You Are Planted"

Black Nore Review: "Passing" and "Louisiana Garden"

The Rainbow Poems: "Uninvited Guest" and "Imperfect Mending"

Forthcoming:

The High Window: "New Kid," "Prom Night," and "Selene"

I would like to express my gratitude to Mark Connors and Gill Lambert and to my fellow members of the Wednesday Poetry Group for their excellent critical feedback and for the warmth of their friendship.

Contents

My Life in Cars   13

I

Bloom Where You Are Planted   17
Braiding   18
Erased   19
Family Photo   20
Permanent Damage   21
Louisiana Garden   22
Calcasieu   23
Mrs M, Our English Teacher   24
Prom Night   25
Mack's by the Tracks   26
Clutching   27
The Last Laugh   28
Joan   29
Rain   30
Crawky Murray   31
Haunted House   32

II.

Plague Saint   35
Plagued   36
Clap for Carers   37
Cotswolds: A Prose Poem   38
Comfort Food   39
Neighbours   40
Webs   41
White Raven on my News Feed   42
Witches Broom and Winter Roses   43
Back to Life   44
New Kid   45

III

Bogotá, Christmas Day 2019	49
Saint Barbara	50
Supping at Emmaus	51
Cliffhanger	52
Daredevil	53
Dark Ghosts	54
Sky	55
Cross Words	56
Plan B	57
Passing	58
Que las hay, las hay	59
Fermenting Imbolc	60
Imperfect Mending	61
Hierogylph	62
He Who Fights and Runs Away	63
Visions, after William Blake	64
Selene	65
Mr Morpheus	66
Fairy Hunting	67
Uninvited Guest	68
Definition	69

My Life in Cars

My first car, a yellow Mustang.
American, smooth, zippy. I didn't name him.
He definitely was a boy.

In Portugal, my second, a microscopic Seat,
baptised Manolito. We navigated curves,
skidded on cobblestones, ferried children.

The next, in Scotland, a red Micra
called the Tibster. Northern Irish number plate.
TIB-6790. A raffish car with verve.

Then an upgrade. Slick black Beemer,
named The Tiburón. Same plate,
different style. Sharklike, dangerous.

Later, in the Sussex countryside,
a 4 x4, the Cloonster, named for George. Silver fox.
I loaded plants, negotiated twisting lanes, made a garden.

Now in London, a sedate silver Skoda, Tweedledee.
My partner's got a twin. That's how we roll!
Just like the Beckhams, darling. Part of the brand.

I

Bloom Where You Are Planted

I made a garden by the sea,
northern Portugal. Roses bloomed for me,
shielded by stone walls
from blasts of silver wind.

I made a garden up on Skye.
Crofter's cottage. They'll say *a woman
came from the mist. She planted two giant trees.*
Sequoias. I was never one to think small.

I made a city garden by a black heath
where plague victims were interred.
Cascades of yellow flowers.
Blood and bone are good for soil.

I made a garden in the Sussex countryside,
cloaked the house in roses. Grew grapevines.
Filled it with memories, children's laughter,
learned to live with darkness.

I made a London garden. Weeded out old sadness,
threw out decay. Planted bold bursts of flowers,
draped walls in blooms and scent.
Grew temporary happy roots.

Nothing lasts forever.
My mother used to say,
Bloom where you are planted.

Braiding

In a distant Southern parlour.
I comb Grandmother's straight black hair.
People always said she might have Indian blood
Where did all these wrinkles come from?
For goodness sake, I answer. *You're eighty!*
It's okay to have a few.

Now the light streams through the window
in the Sussex countryside. I sit upright.
My granddaughter combs my hair.
It used to be dark gold but now is white.
It feels so strange to think that I am old.
You're beautiful, she says.

Erased

To my mother.

Ladies never work outside the home.
~~I could have been a primary school teacher. I love children, and could have had a regular income.~~

I married a lovely farmer. He took me dancing. We had a perfect life, with servants and bridge games. He never spoke of financial problems.
~~My husband blew his brains out and left me with two small children. We walked in and found his headless body on the bathroom floor. He had embezzled money from his family's firm.~~

I fell in love again and married a year later.
~~My second husband was a very wealthy man and I thought he could provide for my children and me. Besides, he was very good-looking.~~

He lost his money and had a breakdown. I had to go out to work as a stenographer.
~~This is not what I signed up for. Men are supposed to provide for their family. A married lady's place is in the home.~~

When my second husband died, I tried to cope.
~~He should have left me with financial security. How dare he leave me here alone.~~

Indoor voices. A lady never shouts, never complains. Raised voices are so vulgar.
~~I want to scream and scream and scream.~~

Family Photo

White house with columned porch.
In the centre, grandmother in wicker chair.

Behind her, my daddy holds me in his arms.
His stillness has a swagger. My mother's sitting on the steps,

hands clasped demure around her knees.
Grandfather stands apart, silent, dour.

Aunts flutter, swathed in soft white linen.
Tow-headed cousins squirm and scowl.

Grandfather died soon after.
My father lost his fortune and his mind.

Enclosed in sepia, blinded by the Southern sun
they cannot see what's looming.

Permanent Damage

My mother wanted a daughter with blonde ringlets.
My hair was wild and straight. She marched me off
to the beauty parlour. "Odile," she drawled in honeyed tones,
"can you give this child a permanent?"

Odile put in bristled rollers, stabbed me with bobby pins,
slapped acrid purple goop over my scalp,
 the smell so strong it scorched my lids.
Like a doomed saint, I endured the fumes

for what seemed forever.
Then Odile lathered, rinsed, dried.
In the mirror I saw a head,
twisting gorgon mane, cold burning eyes.

Louisiana Garden

A big white-columned house   By the back door a banana tree, leaves clattering in tropical breezes   A bed of camellias, fleshy-petaled and scentless, with names like Pink Debutante and Purple Dawn   Black loamy earth where I dIg for worms, bait to catch fish   One night I leave my teddy on the screen porch where he dies of mildew, black fungus spreading over face and ears Our gardener Hay tends to flowers   His wife Corinne takes care of me One morning they aren't there   Standing behind the bamboo hedge I overhear my mother's soft drawl   *Corinne stabbed Hay last night   Caught him with another woman*   I turn away, line up my dolls against the wall   wonder who will cook our dinner.

Calcasieu

I remember river summers.
young wild things whooping war,
we swing out on vines over coiled brown water
splash yelling into clouds of rainbow light.

People have been known to drown
in these dark waters when they flail
against the roiling hissing current.
But Louisiana children know the score.

>   To keep afloat you just lie back into the river,
>   rest into those rippling arms
>   ride her currents in white laughter,
>   know she bears you where she will.

Mrs M, Our English Teacher

She walked around in front of the class,
fondling her cleavage, lips pursed, bubble-gum pink.
The only play we read was *Macbeth*.
She made big tough farm boys from the Louisiana rice fields
memorise soliloquies. Shuffling from one foot to the other,
head down, they would recite, *'If it 'twere done when 'tis' done
'twere well it were done quickly.'*
You can say that again. Torture.

She did teach us grammar, that's for sure.
She barked, *Verb! Subject!*
pointed with her stick as we drew diagrams
of sentence structure on the board, chalk spiderwebs.
Obsessed with conspiracy theories,
she said Eisenhower and Martin Luther King
were Communist agents. *They are Of the Enemy!*
Evil teenagers, we snickered under our breath.

Mrs M is of the enema.
A sentence in which she was both
subject and object.

Prom Night

The gym is festooned with paper streamers,
orange and black. School colours.
Teacher/chaperones lurk in the bleachers, glower.

My date is a rice farmer in a stiff linen jacket.
He brings me a corsage of pink roses.
I give him a pink boutonniere.

In half light, we jitterbug to Little Richard,
wish we were on a Surfin' Safari.
gyrate to Chubby Checker.

I wear pink tulle, ruched around the neckline.
Underneath, hooped petticoat, Scarlett O'Hara sway.
We feel so suave and glamorous. Redneck royalty.

Mack's by the Tracks

There once was a low dive
in Jackson, Mississippi.
Mothers warned their daughters:

> *Whatever you do,*
> *Don't go to Mack's by the Tracks.*
> *Not the sort of place for Nice Girls.*

Of course we made a beeline.
Mack's was timber-clad.
Motorbikes leaned against the porch.
Walls rattled when the trains went past.

Inside, a billiard table ringed by shady men
in pools of dark. In one corner, a juke box
flashing neon shades. We put in quarters,
summoned up Full Frontal Elvis:

> rocked jailhouses,
> conjured hound dogs
> dreamed of hunks of burning love

in magenta, green, blue pulses.
We jitterbugged, twirled, danced slow jives.

Clutching

Some reach out for a piece of you,
handful of ash to scatter
on the mountain wind.

Others want to be you,
live your life
to keep you here.

I try to capture you
with nets of words,
but you elude me.

I can hear your mocking laughter
threaded silver on the breeze,
fading as you float away.

The Last Laugh

Reader, she married him.
He paid court to her younger sister Marie,
flighty redhead who wore feather boas,
drank pink gin. He promised he would take her off
to gay Paree. She turned him down,
said that not for all his millions would she spend
a single night with That Old Man. He turned his attention
to her older sister Cris, the plain one, virtuous.
She said yes, but on honeymoon they only got to Tupelo.
She was a good wife to him. Soon he died.
Cris took over his bank, tripled deposits,
traveled the world.

She who laughs last

Joan

Her bones are glowing charcoal.
Her blood boils scarlet.
Her flesh crackles. Fingers flash spirals of sparks.

Incandescent woman. Blazing in the flames,
her power is to know
she will survive this crucible,

come out from the fire a sword,
tempered, stronger than the brightest steel.

Rain

The road ahead is slick and dark.
Wipers shush shush shush
On the radio, soft voices tell tales
of *love, oh love oh careless love,*
broken hearts for sale
Red lights in front of me
spatter arterial drops against the glass
scatter loss in glowing ruby fistfuls.

Crawky Murray

Crawky was an only child. She had no stepsisters
      angry because their father died,
      stepbrothers lonely and afraid,
      a mother torn in two.
Crawky hated dresses, dolls,
wore silver suits of shining armour.

When something naughty was done
      scuffing mother's high-heeled clock clock shoes,
      throwing stones at greenhouse windows,
      stealing cookies from the kitchen.
Crawky was up to no good.
I of course was miles away.

My imaginary pigtailed friend feared nothing:
      not the maid who told stories,
      of the Waterhead Boy
      who came for wicked children in the night.
Crawky's teeth glowed in the dark,
snarled at marauders.

Haunted House

My grandparents' house was once a hotel.
Grandfather cut it in two, moved it on rollers
 to where it now rests, white gingerbread galleon
floating in full sail across rippling Louisiana fields.

We children used to hunt for treasure left in closets
by passing hotel guests, found none.
Ghosts lurked in corners, sad old stories
 of grandmother's flirtation with a handsome chorister.

She always denied it. Still, my grandparents endured,
wedlocked for forty years in silence.
Please ask your father to pass the salt.
Please tell your mother I've gone out.

The air inside the house was thick and dark.
Anger seethed, cracked like pistol shots.

II.

Plague Saint

In Rome, he's fair-haired Rocco
framed in gold leaf. He holds a pilgrim staff.
His cloak is scarlet, his hose bright blue.
On his head, a jaunty hat.

In Spain, he's known as Roque.
He looks out, pallid, haughty
his greyhound at his feet.
In his hand, a loaf of bread.

In France, they call him Roche.
Eyes haunted, coquettish, almost boastful,
he points at a pustule on his white knee.
An angel floats nearby.

In Ireland, he's named Roch.
In stone, he stands atop an altar,
Small dark silhouette. He flickers
in flames from votive candles

Perhaps it's fitting in a plague
The designated saint is a shape-shifter
flowing effortless across borders.

Plagued

The air crackles with electronic noise.
Casualties rise, markets plummet.
Demagogues scoff.
Nothing to see here.
Just take it on the chin.

In supermarkets, people shove and scuffle.
We whistle in the dark, tell ourselves
Only one percent. The seas are rising.
In Africa, a plague of locusts.
Australia's ablaze.

I tell myself there have been plagues before
and the world's still turning. Still, this time
there seems to be a trailing off,
a slow silencing,
a dark finality.

Clap for Carers

Leafy London street,
Genteel, Victorian, sedate.
Dusk has fallen.
All is silent, eerie.
Then we emerge, stand on front steps
Roars of applause ripple to sky.
People drum on rubbish bins,
bang on pans, smile and wave
across the street, nod to next door.

Though we are in isolation
I have never felt such closeness.

Cotswolds: A Prose Poem

We walk around the old market town. Fortunes were made here from wool. Now Japanese tourists follow in the footsteps of Hirohito, who came here on a state visit. They wander around buying tourist tat, Union Jacks, nodding bulldogs. Masked, we pass one another far apart, intricate plague minuet. The bridge arches across the river. Golden light glances off the stones. We go into the ancient church, burn a votive candle. In the churchyard, old stones jut out at angles. We read *John Clinkard died of plague, 1497.*

Comfort Food

I give thanks for

> The orange crunch of carrots.
> Apples, cored, sliced.
> Leafy salads.
>
> Strong black coffee. Double espresso.
> Good white wine, chilled in the glass.
> Cold beer. Champagne bubbles.
>
> Ice cream, salted caramel if poss.
> Berry crumbles. Lemon tart.
> Pizza La Reine. Queenly indeed.
>
> Doritos. Enough e-numbers to pickle King Tut.
> Cheese. Ah cheese!
> Elasticated waistbands.

Neighbours

Over the fence his head goes
boing boing boing. Ben, my next-door neighbour
nine years old, on his trampoline.
Near us, sirens wail. A hospital's nearby.
Ben waves and grins. I say, *Hi neighbour.*
He's good at many things.

When food was hard to get
his mum would go out to the shops
and bring us things. She's teaching him at home.
We'd get a bill from Ben, artist-accountant,
 with rows of sums, drawings of ice cream,
suns, apples, smiley faces.

Webs

I remember baking cookies
two small bodies pressed
warm against my arms.

Now, their faces flicker.
The eldest asks *Where are you?*
She's cross. This is not fun.

I smile. *I'm here in London.*
What are you up to?
They show off Lego towers.

I read with the littlest,
an online book for six-year-olds
Sometimes I spell things out for her

kuh-ah-tuh

She cries 'Cat!' Sometimes she drifts off,
loses her place. My finger is not there
to point the way. But she's a stubborn little thing,

keeps on wrestling with the words.
we know together
we will reach the end.

White Raven on my News Feed

When it all begins to get to me
        mad politicians
        children in cages
        plagues, climate meltdown

I scroll through images:
        cuddly puppies
        fluffy bunnies
        cats being cats

        A white raven. The caption says:

        In First Nation indigenous tradition
        The White Raven is a Bringer of Light,
        A Trickster, or an Omen that
        the End of the World is nigh.

I sip my coffee. Perhaps it's all
a cosmic prank designed to flush out flaws
an omen of apocalypse and endtimes

a sign we'll be borne skyward on translucent wings
fly triumphant toward the light.

Witches Broom and Winter Roses

This year is nearly over.
We walk arm in arm,
hear the sound of sirens
incessant background dirge.

On our street, three cases.
One next door, one across the way.
Another, three doors down.
No dead so far.

Stubborn Pollyanna, I look for signs
of hope, coded messages that we will
evade the lightning bolts, keep walking
till we reach the other side.

On a bush near our house,
a bright red winter rose
has survived the frost.
On a tree, I see what seems a nest.

A friend tells me it's a growth
called witches' broom. I find this
reassuring. Witches put brooms
by the door to keep those inside safe.

We'll be breathing come next spring.

Back to Life

I wonder what would happen
if Lazarus came back to life
in a sunlit Sussex pub.
Would he be tentative, whiffy,
cloaked in tomb perfume?

He might rock up, place his order,
toast his comeback with a glass
of Harvey's glinting amber.
Black loam clinging to his funeral robes,
he stands a round, chats with local punters.

We watch him from the garden,
sit blinking in the sunlight.
newborn kittens. The valley yawns,
stretches out below us, fields rippling green,
air humming, strung tight with bees.

New Kid

The new kid on the block has a weird name.
Not sure if they're a boy or girl. Omicron sounds like
a tech startup, a strange new deity, a souped-up sports car.

I try to size them up, wonder what they'll look like.
Will Omicron be an inoffensive girlie, poking her nose
in everybody's business? A bore, but harmless really.

Though Omicron might well turn out to be a bloke,
a bruiser, a toxic macho ASBO thug
who breaks through walls, perhaps a killer?

III

Bogotá, Christmas Day 2019

We walk around the central square.
Families stroll, arms linked.

The blare of carols from a shop
proclaims joy to the world.

I smile at you. *What a peaceful place.*
You nod. We walk up to a church,
read the blue plaque on the wall:

> *1814. Ocho soldados españoes fusilados en este lugar*
> *por las fuerzas del general Simón Bolívar .*
> *Viva Colombia! Viva la Revolución!*

Gunshots dance in sunlight.
Ghosts ripple in the air.

Saint Barbara

On the wall, a painting. Italian, 17th –century.
A tower with three windows. In the centre,
 A Saracen with scimitar, a woman on her knees.
I think about the studio of the Master who produced it,
Late Renaissance assembly line.

One apprentice paints the threat of hands
that grasp the woman's hair. Another paints
the swirls of cloth that shroud the woman's face.
Another daubs louring thunderclouds
and jagged lightning spears.

My mind turns to provenance.
It was bought in Portugal
from people fleeing revolution.
Before that, owned by an industrialist.
Before him, a slave trader.

Haunted by the hands that made it,
the female martyrdom it pictures,
the gaze of those who owned it
the dark origins of their money.
I like to think of Barbara as patron saint of artillery

Bursting through the canvas surface
Hurling bolts, blasting all to cinders.

Supping at Emmaus

The two disciples walk toward Emmaus
with heavy tread. They left their Master
torn and broken, sealed in stone by Roman hands.

As night falls, they ask a stranger they encounter
on the way to come and dine with them.
In the village inn, the lights are dim.

The landlord and his wife lay out solid fare,
prepare to leave them. Suddenly
the stranger blazes bright, then ripples back

into the blackest dark. Luke and Cleophas blink,
transfixed, ask themselves how it can be
that boundaries between dimensions are so porous,

how divine beauty
can transcend the night, shimmer
into dusty worlds of bread and sweat and aching feet.

Cliffhanger

We hold on for all we're worth
clinging by our fingertips.
Sometimes we just can take no more
let go, cartwheel into oblivion, float off into sky.
Or bounce off a ridge that breaks our fall,
escape bruised, scratched, in one piece.
Or crash down on the rocks,
shatter, pick our pieces up, laugh,
patch the fragments back together, better.

Daredevil

The mule is standing there,
all bones and flies,
 tail flicking, eyes askance.

I climb up the rails, breathe deep.
Someone dares me
jump from the fence!

I leap, land astride the bucking beast,
fly through space in perfect arc,
crash down into a briar patch.

To this day I bear the scars,
my badge of honour,
light lacework on my thigh.

Dark Ghosts

Some were packed head to tail to maximize
the shipper's profit. Some died, cargo jettisoned,
Their seaweed hair floats in the waves,
veils the phosphorescence in their eyes.
In storms their voices echo in the wind,
threaded thick with lightning bolts. Traders unloaded others,
auctioned them, sent them to chop cane, pick cotton. Some bore
white babies branded with their owners' faces.
Most didn't make old bones.

They haunt the soil and sea. One night they cluster in dark water
by the dock to give a fellow ghost the welcome he deserves.
Headfirst, he sails through air, sinks below the waves. Around him
trails a cloak, kick-dented bronze, covered in paint dyed scarlet as
their blood. He cannot meet their gaze.
The old slaver tried to wash his hands,
exorcise dark ghosts with charity,
good works. The sea, the air reverberate
 with ghostly thunder, growing louder.

Sky

I reach up and touch the sky.
Soft and cold on my fingertips,
It gives way like wet blue cardboard.

I poke a finger through it…
Through the ragged gap an angel falls.
He is not best pleased.

What the hell are you doing?
He looks like my high school principal,
all sagging cheeks and greasy hair.

His wings are mangy. I say to him,
*I want to know if there is something up there
that makes sense.* He looks down to my face.

Silly girl, he says.

Cross Words

My mother used to ask me
*What's a three-letter word starting in q
for a cactus found in Saudi Arabia?*

This usually happened when I was talking
to my friend Margie, or had my nose
buried in a book. I gritted my teeth,

though of course I never voiced my rage,
just raised an eyebrow, heaved a sigh.
Passive-aggression, served up Southern style.

Now sunlight streams through a London window.
With a crossword on my lap, I scratch my head,
ask what's *a river at Aviemore?*

It's said that in old age
We turn into our mothers.
They get us in the end, they do.

Plan B

In the top drawer, painkillers
for aching joints, aging knees.
Molting post-its. Vitamins.

In the second, a brass bracelet.
Bag of earrings. Ropes of pearls.
A vial of French perfume.

Bottom drawer. Important papers.
NHS card, driving licence.
Three passports if I need to flee.

Passing

We haven't *lost* the dead.
We know exactly where they are.
Scattered in a park;
six feet under in a sunlit meadow.

They don't *pass away*.
The holes left by their absence
always hover, darkness
at the edges of our vision.

They aren't *late*.
They've moved beyond time,
shooting through the night sky,
comets trailing stardust.

Que las hay, las hay

I like to see myself
floating far above the clouds
of obtuse ignorance,
superstition.
And yet that's not entirely true.

In Spain, they know a thing or two.
They say *las brujas no existen*
Pero que las hay, las hay.
Witches don't exist,
but there are definitely a few around.

Fermenting Imbolc

Radio drifts over from next door *love oh love oh careless love* I
clomp back to the porch, wipe dark mud from my soles,
brew a cup of tea, sit by the fire. In the other chair, I see Brigid's
come to call. Daughter of a poet, she glows radiant
in the shadows, shoulders shielded by sheep,
head framed by floating creatures. Her cloak is red.
It's said she knew how to turn water into beer.

Grass squelches underfoot. A squirrel frisks,
chitters on the back fence. In the distance,
siren banshees wail, a dog barks.
Secaturs weigh, cold metal in my hands. I lean over,
prune bare rose stems   satisfying snick snick
On dark stems shaken by the storms,
tiny buds begin to sprout. The days are longer now.

Imperfect Mending

You bring me your green jumper.
Between the shoulder blades.
the moths have left a stab scar.

I fish for dark green thread.
There's not an exact match
but one that's near enough.

I thread the needle, bind the edges up
as best I can. The join will show.
It will have to do for now.

Beauty doesn't lie in seams
we cannot see, but how our gaps
are stitched together,

warding off dark cold.
I hope it keeps you warm.

Hierogylph

Grass. Maybe it's salad, slaw for cows,
or hair bursting out from graves,
something to be combed
into prim suburban stripes.

Trees. Maybe they're aspiring to be ships one day,
when they're grown, or shade-spreaders shielding us from sun
or rods to hang a child's swing or a poem, or an avian time-share,
sparrows darting in and out.

Flowers. Maybe they're children's faces nodding, nodding,
or splashes of yellow sunlight, rippling in the distance
or tarty grenades of thick dark red rose scent
or a buzzy fast-food joint for bees

Maybe they're just **grass**, **trees**, **flowers**.

He Who Fights and Runs Away

Sun streams through the window.
Outside, sudden cacophony of crows.

What on earth I think. In the back garden,
I see a plump ginger cat,

draped in the branches of the chestnut tree.
Black feathered shapes swoop,

screech dark avian imprecations.
declare unrelenting blitzkrieg.

The cat goes still, then shimmers
down the branch, arches boneless

 through air, fades into the bushes,
lives to face another day.

Visions, after William Blake

I don't talk about it much.
Straitjackets do not suit me.

For most, they're just white petals falling,
spiralling in the wind. That isn't what I see.

London skies are thick with angels,
wings fluttering, feathers falling on dark roofs.

Their haloes hover as they somersault
among the stars, glowing sparks of light.

Selene

Above black roofs she hovers, unearthly.
I am tempted to let out a howl.
Such things are not encouraged
on this sedate London street.

She has her own dark side,
her realm of secret screams
and spells where she-wolves roam free,
drawing magic from the night.

They say that she reflects the sun.
I don't believe it for a bit.
Selene glows with her own light,
coin suspended in city sky,

shedding waves of silver power
on staid Victorian roofs.
She doesn't need Apollo's rays
to give her purpose, meaning.

Mr Morpheus

I have another lover.
He's very discreet,
comes by to pay
his evening calls

Sometimes, he plays hard to get,
eludes me, keeps his distance.
I toss and turn in longing.
But when his black velvet weight

presses down on me insistent,
surging, I surrender sated
by his dark embrace,
better than the wildest dreams.

Fairy Hunting

Our house looks out on ancient woodland.
The girls and I go hunt for fairies.
*Look under branches, arching roots
under hornbeam trees* I tell them.

The eldest frowns. *But we can't see them.*
I explain that eyes don't work for fairy-spotting.
The winged ones speak to us,
voices in our minds if we believe.

We walk down winding foxpaths,
see a stirring in the trees,
a dancing swarm of light.
There they are cries the littlest.

Uninvited Guest

We sit around a table.
All of us are getting on.
One's wheezy. Two have cells gone rogue.
A fourth is under pressure.

There's an uninvited guest.
We try hard to pretend
he isn't there. He peers through cracks
in conversation, lurks in dark corners.

He tugs insistent at our sleeves.
Rude, really. Not our sort at all,
this boring party crasher.
We do our best to silence him,

fend him off with champagne flutes,
sparkling conversation. We talk
of future plans, foreign holidays.

Let's face the music and dance.

Definition

To D on Valentine's Day, 2022

For you love is a verb
not a flowery lace-fringed noun.
>you put out vitamins and the papers in the morning
>send me messages dotted with fat hearts
>give me your arm to lean on when we take a stroll
>light the fire to keep me from the cold.
>do quizzes, FaceTime with the family
>take the girls to Christmas carols, go Lion Kinging.

You're not a bloke for flowery language.
But every single day you show me in so many ways
you love me by all the things you do
When I make lists of all the blessings in my life
way up there at the very top
is you.

About the Author

Susan Castillo Street is Harriet Beecher Stowe Professor Emerita of American Studies, King's College London. Originally from the American South, she has lived in Europe for most of her adult life, first in Portugal, then in Scotland and now in England. *Braiding* is her fifth poetry collection.

www.ingramcontent.com/pod-product-compliance
Lightning Source LLC
Chambersburg PA
CBHW021025090426
42738CB00007B/910